The Dragons Backbone

The cover picture shows two men working on the *Dragons Backbone*, as they
raise water to irrigate the fields (see p. 178)

Portraits of Chengdu People in the 1920's

by

William G. Sewell
Drawings by Yu Zidan

William Sessions Limited
York, England

Card ISBN 1 85072 006 1
Hard ISBN 1 85072 007 X

Printed in Bembo Typeface
by William Sessions Limited,
The Ebor Press, York, England.

Dedication

William Sewell died in January 1984 at the age of 85. He had hoped to arrange for this book to be published during his life time and to dedicate it 'to the Europe China Association and to all those who strive for greater understanding among the people of the world'. His family and friends have fulfilled his wish in affectionate remembrance.

List of Illustrations

Foreword

Much to our surprise, towards the end of 1924, my wife and I found ourselves in China. We had been married a year or two and had both fallen under the spell of our Chinese college friends, who urged us to follow them across the world and teach in China. Rather adventurously we decided to do just that. Moreover, we were not at one of the more usual places along the coast or on the Yangtse River (or Changjiang, Long River, as it is now called) but in the far west of the country, at the walled city of Chengdu, the capital of Sichuan, a province comparable in size to France.

It was obvious that we must learn Chinese, for in those distant parts few people spoke English. Fortunately, the West China Union University, to which we were attached, had a language school, in which we enrolled as full-time students. The head of the school was an American, but the teachers were all Chinese, forbidden to use any words of English. It was there we met Yu Zidan, 俞子丹, who wrote his romanised name in the old way, Yu Tze Tan. He made the pictures in this book.

At first we knew him only for his ability as a teacher. The Direct Method calls for some skill in acting, and Yu Zidan was superb. He never wearied, even in the very early days of endless repetition: 'We are English, you are Chinese; I want, I do not want; this is a pencil, that is a watch.' I can still see him joyfully raising both thumbs and giving a whoop of triumph when at last we grasped his meaning. Once he was on all fours, giving a credible impression of a tiger, as he taught us to say *fu* in the right tone, instead of using a wrong one which might mean either bran, happiness or even a married woman. His quick response to our whispered guessing in the game of charades betrayed that he knew more English than he admitted.

We always looked forward to the times when it was our turn to be allotted to Mr. Yu. Most of the teachers were good, but he alone had the capacity for conveying so much more than the rudiments of language, telling us the things we needed to know. He guided our behaviour and instructed us in manners: always to give and receive with both hands; to sit in humble seats near the door, until pressed to move higher; to escort guests as they left the house, and never to say goodbye when standing at a higher level than those to whom we were speaking. He told us the proper way to address our elders, and about family customs. We enjoyed the moral stories, such as grandmothers tell children, which he dramatised, taking the parts of leading characters. His face, like his voice, was expressive, passing instantly from one extreme emotion to another. Regrettably, no photograph of him is available.

One day a rather shy Yu Zidan showed us a black and white drawing of a water carrier (reproduced on page 1). When we admired it, he insisted that we kept it. We knew that compensation would be acceptable; and I trust we satisfied conventions by giving to our honourable teacher a gift of nicely calculated value, suited to our relationship and status. We were so delighted with the picture that, every now and then, we were able to buy others from him, augmenting a trifle his 'wood and water', as his rather meagre salary was called.

After we left the language school, I started to teach chemistry in Chinese, which, although very faltering, owed nearly everything, except technical terms, to Yu Zidan. Occasionally we met him, and were able to obtain a few more of his pictures of the people round about and their occupations, in which we were particularly interested. When we went on leave, he brought quite a number to us, which completed our collection. These drawings were all made in the 1920's, although I have a suspicion they sometimes illustrated memories from his own childhood, which reached back into imperial times. We received the first in 1925, and the final batch in 1930.

These pictures contain a wealth of detail, much of it quite minute, which, with the passing of time, may easily be forgotten: indeed, because of the major political and social changes, due to the reorganisation of the country under the People's Republic, much has already gone, as I discovered from Chengdu students now studying in England. Yu was a self-taught artist, and some of the pictures are amateurish, yet he had such obvious delight in the people he depicted that they are a pleasure to see. He gives a sense of reality, and, probably without realising it, has provided us with an important historical record of the lives of the ordinary people who worked in the open shops of Chengdu, or walked the streets selling their wares. When he brought his pictures to me, Yu Zidan would tell me something about the people he had drawn. I have tried to remember his stories, but it was a long time ago: yet, I feel that my comments on the pages that follow reflect in a small way the artist himself, for so much of my early knowledge of China sprang from him.

I left China in 1952, my wife a year earlier, to be with our children in England. We had remained nearly 30 years; but China is a magnet that attracts and keeps many of those who live there. These pictures remain one of our most treasured possessions. They remind us of Chengdu, its people and our Chinese friends, with some of whom we still have contact. I have tried to trace Yu Zidan, but so far have failed. For 30 years letters to Chengdu brought no response. Now, when letters again come and go, further enquiries have not discovered any trace of him. The city itself, however, has been transformed. The wall and many familiar streets have gone; the population has swollen from over half a million to more than four million, and older people have tended to return to villages from which they sprang.

Yu Zidan, like others of our friends, may no longer be alive: yet he indeed lives through the pictures he made. Often I wonder what he might have become if he had received instruction, for he was a born artist. He rubbed his ink-stick with a little water on a slab; then, when he judged the consistency to be correct, he moistened his ordinary Chinese brush-pen in the ink and drew, on small scraps of paper, these Chinese people, so true to life, decorated by the little fancy pieces which he so much loved. Among such conceits I like the dragon's head, at the end of the tailor's pole (page 35). Yu never really understood the significance of perspective, as the illustration of the sugar-cane seller shows (page 109). Yet I have included this because of the wealth of detail.

In my book, *The People of Wheelbarrow Lane* (published by George Allen and Unwin, in 1970), there are over a score of these pictures, now again reproduced. I then wrote rather fancifully about Yu; but, although I did not always stick to basic facts, as I have done here, everything I said was true as an expression of the effect which he had as a counsellor of a young foreigner, new to China, and as a language teacher. His reputation as an accomplished writer of Chinese characters was known in the city. People who wished to present scrolls at weddings, funerals or the important birthday anniversaries of the elderly, often commissioned these from him. This skill of his is reflected in a few of the pictures which he has signed, or to which he has added a title in Chinese.

My special thanks are due to my wife, as together we have looked once again at these illustrations, remembering the days of our youth, and the people among whom we, and our children, lived. I thank also Liao Hongying, friend and colleague of Chengdu days, who has helped me to remember the significance of some of the pictures. Above all, my greatest gratitude is to Yu Zidan himself. This will also be felt by his old pupils, now scattered throughout the world, who owe so much of their understanding of the Chinese language and people to his inspired teaching – a sense of gratitude which, I believe, will also be shared by those who look at these pages.

Kew Gardens   *William G. Sewell*
England

The Water Carrier

WHEN WE TURN THE TAP, water comes without trouble; but for the people of Chengdu every drop they used had to be carried into the house, for at that time they had no piped water. In almost every courtyard there was a well. The very name for courtyard is *tian jing* (天井) heavenly well, for the yards were open to the skies (*tian*). The families who lived round about drew their water from the well, usually assisted by some balancing device, such as a long pole, with a stone tied to the end, which acts as a lever. The character *jing* suggests a central well, with criss-cross paths leading to it from the homes of those who live in the compound. People who lived too far away from a well had to buy their water from a carrier.

Once, a Chinese colleague confessed to a stupid forgery he had committed. Depressed and thoroughly miserable he at last managed to blurt out his story, declaring that he at once felt relief like a water carrier whose buckets had suddenly emptied! A full bucket is very heavy; and to carry a pair is hard labour indeed.

A curved, slightly resilient pole is said to make it easier to carry a heavy load, especially for short distances. The carrier moves quickly in rhythm with the springing pole. Note the conventional hooks which support the buckets. A large leaf is sometimes placed on the surface of the water to prevent splashing; but the experienced carrier manages to jog along with little likelihood of any spilling.

The Furniture Carrier

IF YOU WANTED TO MOVE some of your household chattels there were no furniture vans in the narrow streets of Chengdu. In the 1920's they were only just beginning to think of widening some of the main roads. A carrier had therefore to be summoned, unless the goods were small enough to pack into one of the rather simply made local rickshaws.

It was always amazing to see the way in which even the most difficult articles, such as this rope bed and square wooden table, could be fitted together to make a single load. How to arrange the things often required considerable thought and time, assisted by bystanders who were always ready to give advice, and occasionally to lend a hand to lift the load onto the carrier's back, no doubt thankful it wasn't their own.

In hot weather the carrier was always glad to have a hand free in which to hold a plaited bamboo fan with which to cool his face as he staggered along. No wonder such men are called coolies, for their labour is indeed bitter – *ku li*(苦力).

Homeward Bound

I SUSPECT SHE HAS BEEN to visit her mother-in-law. As the day is ending she must get home with the baby boy she carries on her back in the beautifully made plaited bamboo basket in which he sits. He is wearing an animal hat, so necessary for little boys. Our children used to call them cat-hats! You can see the cat face and sticking-up ears. Any devil passing by, and taking a look, would never imagine it was a little boy; it would go on its way doing no harm.

It isn't really dark yet, but it soon will be. It is difficult to light the lantern on the way, so it is already lit. It is a beautiful lantern, decorated with bats, for bats mean happiness, both being called by the same sound: *fu*. She is fortunate to have such a nice lantern; most people when they went out at night carried torches made of pieces of bamboo rope from the plaited cables used by trackers to pull boats up the river.

Like other married women, her hair is combed back, fastened in a bun. Round her head is a black band of cloth or silk. She carries a local oiled paper umbrella: useful against the Sichuan rain or drizzle.

The dog belongs to her mother-in-law, and has seemingly been on friendly terms with the baby. You didn't take your own dog for a walk in Chengdu: there would have been a fight every few steps with other mongrels guarding their territory. Few dogs were pets: they were watch-dogs and scavengers. I suspect the artist put it in to balance the lantern; but he has drawn one of my favourite pictures.

The Water Buffalo

SQUELCH, SQUELCH – as one by one the feet are moved, with maddening deliberation, in the mud! Prodding the beast's tough hide with the stick, torrents of the most lurid Chinese imprecations, and utter denigration of its parents, fail to make the water buffalo move more quickly as, with a metal tipped plough, it prepares the flooded field for planting rice seedlings.

Planting Rice

IN THE SPRING the fields are flooded and ploughed ready for the rice. The seed is scattered on a small patch, the little green plants appearing after about ten days or a fortnight.

When the seedlings are sufficiently grown they are transferred to the fields: a back breaking job. When a field is completed it is always a marvel that the rows are so straight and parallel with each other. Groups of several people usually worked in a line, moving backwards together as the seedlings were pushed into the mud.

Near one corner of the little earth paths which surround the field there is a gap which is blocked with turf and stones. It is opened to allow water to enter, each farmer having rights, on stated days and at particular times, to use water from the general irrigation channels, which form a network over the Chengdu plain. A branch of one of these channels, crossed by a narrow foot-bridge, runs along beside the rice fields.

The Threshers

AFTER THE RICE HAS GROWN and summer advances, the fields become dry and dusty, while the ripening grain turns a golden-brown. Then comes the day of harvest. The rice is cut by hand; and the sheaves threshed against a wooden trough, at the back of which there is a plaited bamboo mat to prevent loss of grain.

Usually two men thresh together, naked to the waist, trousers rolled up, for it is the hot season of the year. Rhythmically, first one and then the other, they beat the dry sheaves against the tub. Their bodies are yellow with dust, their backs glistening with sweat, their muscles rippling as they work. The women of the farm carry the grain away and spread it on large bamboo mats to dry in the hot sun. The stubble is left. Together with other plant refuse, it is ploughed into the ground after the fields are again flooded in preparation for another crop.

秋成打穀
雪華民國
十九年

Street Puppets

THIS PICTURE NEEDS no explanation. Such shows are the joy of the young, and the young at heart of all ages. The foot, the peeping child, the raised arm, even the hair style, all are expressive.

The familiar story, however, is not so crude as our Punch and Judy. It is about the tiger, which looks so fierce, with glaring eyes. It kills a widow's only son, on whom she is dependant. For this crime the tiger is caught and hauled before the magistrate. He berates it, not so much for killing a man, but for the dastardly crime of making life hard for the old woman. The magistrate, as punishment, orders it to look after her for the rest of her days. Repentant, overcome by the realisation of the wrong it had done, the tiger agrees. It serves her until she dies, providing her with food and money. The tiger mourns at her grave, then wastes away, to reappear in the last scene in the world of ghosts, where it turns out that in some rather obscure way the spirit of the widow's son had, after his death, entered into it. The moral, however, has once more been driven home: that filial children should look after their parents in their old age.

Stilt Walkers

CHENGDU WAS A CITY of hard workers at the period when these pictures were made. There was no piped water, no drains, except open ones in some streets; no gas; electricity was just coming, but for most people not yet for light or power. The countless devices which have transformed our homes and industries were unknown. Many of the inhabitants were illiterate. Together with the rather dull, endless grind were family responsibilities and joys, neighbours with whom to gossip and quarrel, also many simple, natural pleasures, often self-made.

Everyone looked forward to festival days, especially the traditional activities of New Year, to visiting friends, eating the special foods, making pilgrimages to temples, walking on high places, such as the city walls, and the merit of liberating life, returning captured fish to the rivers, and birds to the air. There was Sichuan Opera for those who could afford it, but no regular cinemas, and no radio. People watched the itinerant entertainers who performed in the street, or listened, while sipping tea in the tea-shops, to the story tellers. There were the delights of long twisting dragons which writhed down the streets at certain seasons, also the dancing lions, and acrobats doing daring deeds, like these two funny men on 'high legs'. From the way the artist has drawn them, it is obvious how much he himself appreciated them.

高腳
獅子舞

Spinning Plates

WHEN CHINESE ACROBATIC TROUPES visit Europe, how we all enjoy the lovely girls in their gorgeous silks as they twirl plates, several at a time, dancing and forming amazing figures. This picture tells how it all starts: a boy in a back street, with a dish beside him, hopefully expecting some coppers.

The Peep-show

A PEEP-SHOW: and only a small copper for a view. On top a clapper to attract attention, and a revolving figure. The pictures are in the box on top but when the showman pulls the string they drop into the bottom part. Sometimes every hole has a child peering through it and some are so small they have to stand on tiptoe: there are never sufficient stools for all.

The little boy seems to be enjoying it; although all he sees are drawings of battles long ago, pictures of foreign lands, and perhaps an illustration cut from a foreign magazine.

Monkey Coming

'MONKEY COMING! MONKEY COMING!' the children would excitedly cry when they saw man and monkey coming down the street. They used to visit the local markets and the tea-drinking shops. They were always at temple fairs; and sometimes they were engaged for private parties. Wherever they were, a crowd soon gathered round; and there were sounds of obvious delight and audible whispers of identification as the animal raised each mask before its face, while the keeper told the familiar story of ancient adventure. The monkey, with a little prompting, carried the banners, staves and swords of well-known heroes, jiggling about, acting a part, often with bawdy movements, which brought guffaws from the men, and embarrassed giggles from the women who, in shame, covered their faces with their hands, and watched from between their fingers.

The Blossom Seller

ON A SPRING MORNING, when the prunus first comes out, everyone forgets the winter and looks forward to warm sunshine. The old man with his long basket, ideal for holding flowers, is selling sprigs of prunus blossom *mei hua* (梅花). The flowering twigs are laid at each end of the basket, with azaleas and irises in the middle.

The first popular harbinger of spring has already flowered and is mostly over. It is *la mei* (腊梅), Chimonanthus fragrans, winter-sweet, with its pale yellow, wax-like flowers, and refreshing perfume. It comes at Chinese New Year, and is sought after by every household. Soon, however, it is followed by the more prolific prunus. Most people prefer the red and darker pink varieties, as the colour symbolises happiness and general cheer.

This is one of my favourite pictures, and perhaps of the artist also. Using his finest brush, he has, in the original, coloured each tiny blossom pink, the azaleas red, and the irises pale blue. Otherwise, like all his pictures, the rest is black and white, on a scrap of paper 13 by 10 centimetres in size.

The 'Mo-den' Miss

THIS 'MO-DEN' MISS is being taken home by rickshaw. It looks as though she has been to the Flower Fair to buy some sprigs of pink *mei hua*, beautiful prunus blossom. The Fair is held every spring in an old temple, a short way outside Chengdu. People in their multitudes flock there to buy young trees, shrubs and plants of every description, for their courtyards or gardens, where they grow them in pots or raised troughs, and occasionally in beds, as we in the West grow plants. Some people delight in simply wandering at the Fair, enjoying the crowds and the flowers, eating the snacks offered on small stalls, examining the goods of all kinds laid out for sale: scrolls, pictures, mirrors, singing birds, garishly decorated cold-hot bottles of all shapes and sizes (which we call vacuum flasks), and all manner of novelties, many quite useless, brought from Shanghai.

The girl is probably one of our students. Her hair is cut short in the latest fashion: her two plaits gone. During the winter, as they walk on the campus after classes, the girls have been knitting scarves for themselves and their friends. She is still wearing hers.

The university, like other new buildings, is built with local grey brick. The hedges of prunus round some of the blocks are flowering at this time of year: clouds of enchanting pink blossom against sombre grey. The girl holds the flowers high: they will bring brightness to her rather bare room. She feels her heart lifted, because spring has come.

The Wheelbarrow Ride

THE OLD GENTLEMAN has been to town for the day, wheeled along the narrow paths from the farm by a hired man, or perhaps by his son. He is still wearing his padded winter clothes, and his 'wind-hat' to keep his head warm. If he has bought a few things they will be in the basket behind him, but chiefly he is pleased because he has obtained some of the flowers of spring, a spray of prunus blossom, *mei hua*, which he holds high.

Wheelbarrows are convenient for narrow country paths, but are not very comfortable to ride in, especially if the road is rough or stony. The solid wood wheels, which are often rimmed with iron, cut up the new roads and were, from time to time, banned in the cities because of the ruts they made. Attempts were made to obviate this by making wider wheels and by nailing rope to the rim. The man who pushes the barrow supports the weight by a rope from the ends of the shafts, which passes over his shoulders. When a very heavy load of goods is being carried, a second man in front helps by pulling with a rope.

Carrying the Kitchen 'Tablets'

THERE WAS ALWAYS some interesting sight in the city streets: a bride being carried to her wedding, or a funeral procession. Through the open shutters of the shop-houses there were frequently religious rites to be seen, mixtures of Confucian, Daoist and Buddhist traditions, conducted by priests in their coloured robes. Sometimes there were special things to be carried along the crowded roads: tablets with ancestral or religious connections, gifts for birthdays of the elderly or for weddings, photographs of the deceased, all manner of things, for little was private and so much was shared. These were the occasions when men were hired to carry, as the two in the picture are doing.

The articles are carried on a wooden frame, painted red with patterns in gold or black. If there are gifts to be carried, they are left unwrapped so that all may see how magnificent they are, and marvel at the wealth and generosity of the giver. At important weddings the groom and his family may send to the bride a procession of 20 or more of these loads of presents, which my students assured me could be hired for the occasion.

From our picture it seems that someone has been having trouble in the kitchen, which has been rebuilt and the kitchen god is being re-installed. Three incense sticks burn before a tablet dedicated to Heaven and Earth, the ancestors and the teacher-sages. The smaller tablet to the right, calls, in Daoist phrase, on Highest Heaven, the Kitchen God, and the Kitchen Stove – the symbol of the family's existence.

In the original the artist has coloured the ribbon and the two candles red – increasing the expectation of good fortune.

Street Entertainer

THE PEOPLE FLOCK OUT OF THEIR SHOPS on to the street to watch
performances like this. The man waves swords and daggers in a seemingly
dangerous manner, likely to injure if not kill himself. He ties himself up in
a complicated network of cord from which release seems impossible.
Then, in a flash, he is free – to the enjoyment of the laughing crowd, even
though all but the youngest know it is a trick.

The Blind Medicine Seller

THIS BLIND MAN, feeling his way with his stick, hopes to sell a few of the odds and ends he keeps in his box. Wisely, having learnt from bitter experience, he keeps the box covered, as he knows there are people not averse to stealing his things. However, you can see what he is offering for sale, through the little peep holes covered with glass. Probably among his wares will be needles and thread, face powder and rouge, and common herbal medicines as well.

Life is not easy for those who are blind. Some are skilled in crafts such as plaiting bamboo. Sometimes one can see on the street a string of blind men, each with his hand on the shoulder of the person in front, being led by a small sighted child.

The Tailor

THE TAILOR IS BLOWING on the charcoal in his flat-iron to make it glow. When it is hot enough he will iron the cloth on which he is working. On the table are his scissors and a cord which, when dipped in yellow powder and flicked on the cloth, leaves a straight line along which he can cut. There is also a small ruler and a thimble he wears on his thumb. On his head is a round hat, such as all save country folk and labourers usually wear: the button on top is black, but is red for a wedding or happy occasion, and white when in mourning. He is wearing cloth shoes, and is dressed in a suitable way for the proprietor of a small shop.

He sits at his work on a trestle-seat; these are normally made the same length as a side of the usual square wooden tables. The newcomer soon learns that if he sits on the very end he will quickly find himself on the floor, unless someone is already seated further along.

The completed garments on the pole are waiting for customers to collect them. I suspect that the tailor enjoys, as much as I do, the dragon's head at the rod's end.

The Street Barber

HAIRCUT? No! not for this man. He is having his head shaved; so it must be summer time. The little box of implements is a convenient seat, and there is an arm rest too. These make one end of the barber's load as he moves down the street, to see if anyone else wants a haircut or shave. At the other end of his pole, he strings the hat-stand, delightfully ornamental, and with a mirror. In the tub there is water, in case the client needs a shampoo.

In one of the little drawers he keeps a tiny brush and a scraper to clean out the ears – so soothing, my students used to tell me; but, having listened to my medical colleagues, I felt it too risky to try.

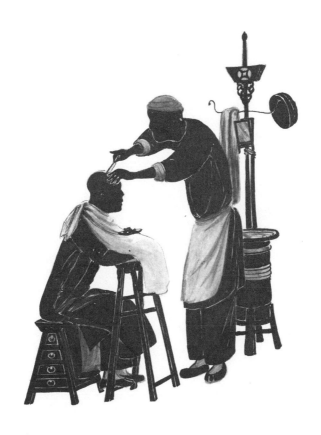

The Barber's Shop

THERE WERE HAIRDRESSERS SHOPS in Chengdu, with locally made chairs and equipment, mostly rather crude imitations of styles from the coast. Note the foreign scissors and clippers, the bottle of oil, the small spray and large brush. When I needed a haircut I did not go to a barber: he came to me. His arrival was the signal for a ritual to start, prescribed by the god of hygiene, whom foreigners were considered to worship, the Chinese not so much. The cook's wife brought a wash-face-bowl, and into it the barber placed scissors, comb and clippers. Then the cook arrived with a kettle and poured boiling water into the basin, while the household stood around silently watching.

The barber's profession calls for no vows of secrecy; but gives a unique opportunity for endless gossip. I learnt amazing things about those who lived in the lane outside the University campus, and about my colleagues on the staff. I often wondered what they heard about me.

The Pedicure

IF YOU HAVE MONEY AND LEISURE, you may have attention given to your feet. You relax with a cigarette and bowl of tea while your toe nails are cut and feet cleaned up. I cannot remember any of my Chinese friends complaining of corns. Both men and women wore cloth shoes without heels; and the men especially liked straw sandals, such as were used by the workers in city and country. It was my western colleagues, with their leather shoes, who developed corns. However leather shoes, in the latest styles from the coast, were at that time beginning to arrive in Chengdu. Officers in the army wore boots made of leather, some locally tanned; but the soldiers had sandals of straw, with coloured pom-poms over the big toe. They carried spares in case of need while on duty.

China's major foot problem had been the binding of little girls' feet; so that, throughout life women were crippled, hobbling as they walked. Once deformed and broken, there was no cure; the feet had to remain bound, often causing increased discomfort in old age. A sad sight was to see better-off women, with tiny feet, wearing normal shoes, which they padded to hide their deformity, yet all too apparent when they walked. Foot binding is now entirely a thing of the past. Soon it will be quite without meaning to say: 'It stinks like Mrs. Wang's foot bandage,' which was used to describe actual bad odours, but more usually in a figurative sense about corrupt practice.

The Bird Vendor

THERE WAS NO MORE PLEASING SIGHT than two old men airing their birds. They would hang the cages on nearby trees, if possible in sunshine, away from cold winds. Then sitting not far away, they would whistle and make bird-like sounds to encourage their pets, discussing in friendly rivalry the songs of the birds. On the old wrinkled faces, there was often a look of quiet satisfaction it was moving to see. Several different kinds of songsters were sought after, but most popular was the Sichuan bulbul, with its thrush-like song. A great achievement by some of the experts was to bring an empty cage, and opening the doors have the birds fly from one cage to the other.

In many courtyards could be seen at least one handsome parrot, chained by its leg to the perch. Some birds, with patience, could be taught to speak, often saying: 'Girl, girl! Make tea,' at which, the children will tell you, the little bondmaids, who at one time served the rich families, would run for the kettle. To the newcomer at Language School, it was always a shock to discover that even parrots could speak in good Chinese.

Birds are often kept in square cages, simpler than those the bird vendor is selling. However, if you already have a cage, he will sell you a bird to put in it.

Spinning Cotton

FACTORIES HAD NOT YET COME TO CHENGDU, and many crafts were conducted chiefly as small family concerns, sometimes providing extra employment for the women. This rather elderly lady, with tiny feet, is spinning cotton. As she turns the big wheel, it rotates the bobbin on which the new thread is wound. As the work was done in homes, from which the upright wooden shutters, fronting on the street, were removed during the hours of daylight, it was always interesting to see what was being done, and to gossip a little with the workers. There always seemed to me a touch of magic in the way the tuft of cotton, which the spinner held in her hand, constantly twisting with thumb and fingers, vanished, so that she had to reach for more from her basket. When they let me try, there was delighted laughter when I failed to get any thread at all, confirming that foreigners were really rather stupid folk, unable to do the simplest things.

Fluffing Cotton – 1

COTTON IS GROWN IN SICHUAN; and is used raw, or spun as thread and woven into cloth. The unspun cotton is used to pad clothing, needed in cold weather as the houses are unheated, except for charcoal braziers, usually in the middle of a room. Overcoats were not worn; but the elderly often carried little baskets, fitted with a small sand tray on which charcoal glowed to keep their fingers warm.

The raw cotton required fluffing up; and after use the padding becomes matted and hard and, especially in the case of children, dirty. It has to be removed from the clothing or bed quilts, often washed and dried, then fluffed up again.

Fluffing cotton is an expert job; and requires a special instrument which the old man is using. It is supported by a bamboo stick, of just the right flexibility, tied to his back. When struck, the taut wire vibrates, catching up the cotton fibres and also making one of the pleasing sounds heard in China.

After the work is finished the women of the house will be busy, spreading it evenly, and sewing the cotton back into jackets, trousers and quilts.

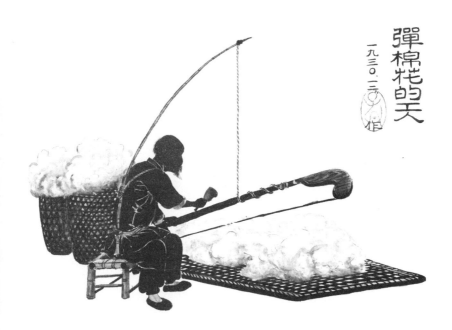

彈棉花的天

一九三〇、二、〇 作

Fluffing Cotton – 2

THIS IS SIMILAR to the preceding picture, but with a younger turbaned man, standing up to fluff the cotton. As he is higher, the cotton has been placed on a plaited bamboo mat, supported on two trestles.

At one time we used beds made with coir fibre ropes, like the one the coolie carried (Illustration p.3). It was so hard that we slept on padded quilts. These gradually got harder, but when re-fluffed were soft and bulky once more. In winter the Chinese people in their padded garments always looked stout; but after fluffing them they looked even stouter.

These two pictures show development in the skill of the artist. The younger man was one of the first he made; but the old man was in the final batch.

The Weaver

THERE WAS NO STREET MORE ATTRACTIVE in which to wander than that of the weavers. Some looms were simple, making the narrow cloth, conveniently used for traditional Chinese clothing; others were more complicated like this one. *Clack, clack*, the noise from so many open shops was almost deafening, as the weavers worked the pedals with their feet, and threw the shuttles to and fro by hand. So quickly did they work that the cloth grew as one watched: sometimes plain, often patterned, with different colours and designs. There was no sense of rush or oppression; the workers seeing a friend, or foreigner, would pause to smile and say a word or two.

This is one of the last pictures the artist made for me. I have never ceased to enjoy the delicacy of line, and accuracy of detail. So many years later, I can still hear the men at work *clack, clack,* continuously *clack, clack*!

木機織縐圖
一九三三年
俞作

Hens for Sale

THE FIRST TIME a Chinese friend came into our home and presented me with a live hen I was quite embarrassed – although I did remember to receive it with both hands. When another visitor followed with a struggling duck I had to call the cook to come to my rescue, for I had hesitations about putting the first gift on our carpet. After all it is very sensible to keep one's food alive until needed, especially in a climate which becomes hot and humid. As we had no refrigerator, the only way to keep food fresh was to put it in the 'wind cupboard' which was made with fine metal mesh, and hung in a breezy place, or alternatively to put it in a basket and lower it into the cool well from which we obtained our drinking water. Another method I have seen is to tie a piece of meat at the end of a very long pole which is raised above the fly level.

When we were to have chicken for supper, the cook bought one a few days or a week ahead from some farmer, like the one pictured, who had brought a load for sale in the city. The legs of the birds were usually tied together with straw, and were handled as the picture shows. After buying a fowl, the thing to do was feed it well for a few days before eating it, sometimes, besides getting a trifle plumper it gave us an egg or two in return for its extra days of life.

The Fishmonger

'ALIVE, ALIVE, OH!' They are swimming about in troughs at the front of the fishmonger's shop: you choose just which you would like. You take them home at the bottom of your basket, weighed down to prevent them jumping out, by putting your vegetables, or other purchases, upon them; or, with a sliver of bamboo through their gills, you can carry them dangling from a couple of fingers.

Restaurants also had troughs of fish. You made your selection, then drank tea, and were served the preliminary dishes while it was being cooked. The Chengdu delicacy was crisp-skin fish. During an anti-foreign period, westerners were accused of bribing students by inviting them to eat this expensive dish. Certainly, anyone would think kindly of a host who fed them on it!

Fish from a distance seems to taste better than local varieties. Some were brought by the Fish Express from rivers several days' journey away. To ensure that the fish should arrive alive and swimming, relays of runners who each carried a pair of containers, like that at the front of the stall, changed the water at rivers as they passed.

The proprietor still wears a queue. When first we reached Chengdu these signs of servitude, imposed on the Chinese by the Manchus, were still occasionally seen, especially among farmers. They were useful tied round the forehead, when doing strenuous labour, to prevent the sweat from running into the eyes: more comfortable than the sweat-bands of straw now used instead.

Rod and Line

THE SOLITARY FISHERMAN with his line and rod always suggests an idyllic escape from the turmoil of life: to sit at the front of a boat, dreamily dozing until a nibble is felt. Around one are mountains and water, which is the Chinese conception of scenery; and one is soothed by the sound of the water gently rippling against the boat's wooden bottom. The man is not separate from the world around him, but is part of it; indeed he has assumed his right place in the great universe itself.

When the day is over, the old man will return home to the small farm where he lives with his married son. The roof, thatched with straw is green with the leaves of gourds; around the door are bright yellow sunflowers. Generously he will offer you hospitality; a trestle to sit on, boiled water to drink, but the picturesque beauty will fade as the reality of heart-breaking struggle takes its place. When the welcoming smiles have vanished, tragedy is reflected from eyes and face; one is surrounded by signs of poverty so extreme that it must be impossibly hard to endure.

The old grandfather was sent out to catch fish for supper. Should he return empty handed the family must be content with plain rice and cabbage.

Cormorants

THESE MEN ARE FISHING with the help of cormorants, whose wings are clipped, so that there is no escape for them from exploitation. Round their necks straw bands are tied, with a nicety which allows them to breathe but does not let them swallow. When a bird has caught a fish it returns to the boat and is helped aboard with the net. It is then made to disgorge into the container which contains water. Finally the bands are loosened so that the birds may have their reward.

When evening comes, the fishermen pull their boats on shore, turn them over and put them, upside down, on their heads. With the black birds (usually four or six of them) clinging rather precariously on top, the men return home to eat some of the fish but selling most of the day's catch.

Basket Fishing

THIS ALWAYS SEEMED a sporting way of catching fish: to be quick enough to pop the tapering bamboo frame over the fish, and then lift it out by hand. This method was sometimes used in slow-moving streams and in rice fields, when they did not wish to empty the field of water and gather up all the fish. At night, lights were sometimes used to attract the fish.

A popular method of fishing along the river banks was to use a net supported on a bamboo frame. This was lowered into the water, then, by the help of a hinge fixed on the bank, raised again with the expectation that there would be fish in the net. I have watched this operation many times, but rarely was there a worthwhile catch.

Calendering

As an acrobatic performance of great dexterity, there were few occupational skills to equal calendering. Cloth, lined with paper covered with white insect wax, or with sheets of highly polished cow skin, was wound by hand on a wooden roller. This was then placed on a slightly hollowed stone slab, over which the rocking-stone was set. The workman, or treadler, mounted the stone, supporting himself by the bamboo poles. By rocking, pressing first with one foot, then the other, the cloth was made to roll backwards and forwards under pressure. Sometimes extra weights were added. When the operation was over the cloth is smooth and has a high lustre.

This rocking-stone looks as though it was new. The artist has put a little message on it, wishing good fortune as they start to use it. Although it looks precarious, like so many traditional skills, it has rhythmic grace and is quite entrancing to watch.

The Riveter

WE TOOK TO CHINA some rather pretty salad plates and found, when we unpacked them, that several were broken. 'Don't worry,' said our friends, 'send for a riveter'. He duly came and sat himself on his little stool in the garden. With his bow he twirled his drill to make minute holes into which he fitted rivets. So skilfully were the pieces put together, that, except by looking underneath, it was difficult to see that the plates had ever been broken.

A Chinese square table seats eight people, and a round one ten or twelve. Rice bowls could be bought individually, or together with vegetable bowls, wine cups, spoons and spice dishes, in sets of ten or more. When as so often happened, a bowl was broken, the riveter would mend it, and so keep the set complete.

The *Shui Gang* Mender

THIS MAN IS REPAIRING one of those articles possessed by every Chinese household, not only in Chengdu but throughout the country. The dictionary calls it 'an earthenware jar to hold water,' a *shui gang*, (水缸). There is no satisfactory English word for it, so westerners in China always use its Chinese name.

Sometimes the *shui gang* gets broken; and then a special riveter is called to repair the damage. With his chisel he makes holes and then inserts his iron rivets, drawing the pieces tightly together. Soon it is once more in domestic use, containing water.

There is a famous story of a broken *shui gang*, which was the first moral tale that the artist, as our language teacher, told us – a familiar story known to every Chinese child. It is about the great historian Sima Guang (司馬光), who lived from 1019 to 1086. His is one of the few Chinese families with a two-character name; Sima, his personal one being Guang. When Sima Guang was a small child, one of his playmates fell into a *shui gang*: it was so big and the boy so small that drowning seemed inevitable. The other children ran away in fear, but Sima Guang, with a sense of responsibility and quick thinking, took a large stone and broke the earthenware jar, so that the water ran out and his little friend was saved.

The Umbrella Maker

UMBRELLAS WERE IMPORTANT IN CHENGDU. This man is putting the finishing touches to one he has just made. Like many craftsmen he is working on the shop floor, so that low stools of wood or bamboo are used. He has already assembled the material for the ribs, the bamboo pieces all neatly shaped and tied together, other slivers glued firmly to the cover. With his brush, held just as the artist shows, he is painting it red, or perhaps green. The cover is made of stout oiled paper. At one time persimmon oil was favoured, but now the commoner wood oil is most frequently used. This wood, or tung oil, comes from the seeds of the *Aleurites cordata*, which grows in Eastern Sichuan. There are also trees in the gardens and courtyards of Chengdu; the poor watch for the coming of its lovely flowers in springtime, for until that time they may not safely shed their winter clothes.

Tending Silkworms

CHENGDU HAS LONG BEEN FAMOUS for its silks, satins and crepe, also for brocades. Silkworms were cultivated on many farms, as a successful means of adding to their income. The eggs, conveniently laid by the moths on paper, are carefully preserved until the mulberry leaves have grown. Then the eggs are warmed, by being carried about by the women in their bosoms, until they hatch. The tiny larvae are transferred to round bamboo trays where they are fed on the leaves. They are tended with care, the women finding chopsticks most useful tools, both for feeding and keeping them clean. The worms grow quickly, their voracious appetites eventually slackening when the larvae are about to turn into chrysalides: from their spinnerets comes the double thread with which they weave the cocoon in which they are imprisoned. In Chengdu the cocoons are mostly bright yellow, the actual colour depending on the kind of leaves the larvae have eaten.

Reeling Silk – 1

SOME SILK COCOONS ARE KEPT until the moth cuts its way out, breaking the threads. The silk moth flutters about but does not fly. After mating, eggs are laid on the coarse paper provided. These eggs are either sold or used for another crop, sometimes two, or even three, being obtained in Chengdu, depending on the availability of mulberry leaves. In southern China, mulberry trees were specially cultivated, so that it was possible to have as many as seven or eight crops of silkworms every year.

Most of the cocoons are used for the fibres from which they are made. They are usually sent to specialist reelers, who boil them to kill the chrysalides, so that no moths emerge, and the threads remain unbroken. Boiling softens the gum which binds the twin fibres, and little fingers are able to find the ends of the threads, which are passed through the loops and then wound on to the big wheel. The fibres from several cocoons are united, held together when cold by the residual gum, to form a single thread.

The girl, whose fingers may get severely scalded, although she uses chopsticks, turns the wheel by means of a foot treadle, while the boy keeps the fire burning.

人工取絲圖 一九三〇子丹作

73

Reeling Silk – 2

ANOTHER EXAMPLE OF THE EQUIPMENT used for reeling silk (see page 72), but in this case managed by a boy alone. As is the custom, it is a young person who is employed, for it requires small fingers (which are often scalded) to find the ends of the silk fibres on the cocoons.

The cocoons, from which the moths have been allowed to emerge, are used to make waste silk. This is used as a padding for the clothing of those who can afford to buy the sheets into which the waste silk has been lightly pressed; the sheets being about 30 cm in length, and a little narrower in width. They are sewn into the garments; they are lighter in weight, warmer and much more elegant than padded cotton. Furs, brought from the mountains west of Chengdu, are also used as linings for winter garments with the fur facing inwards and so unseen – not on the outside as the animals wore them, and as western custom dictates.

Silk Thread

SOMETIMES A THICKER AND STRONGER silk thread is needed, for example to use as warp in weaving. Here the woman is combining several silk threads which have been obtained from the cocoons by reeling. Women in their homes often undertake this work for the larger establishments.

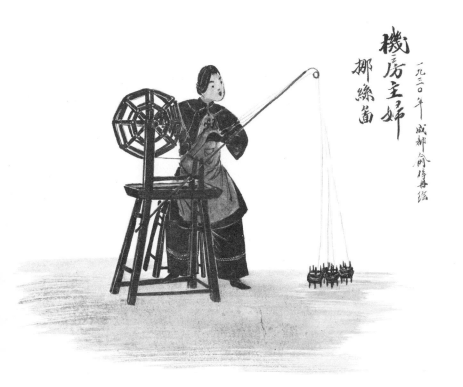

機房主婦
挪絲箇

一九三〇年成都公門侯母繪

77

The Seller of Lucky Charms

SOMEONE MUST HAVE heard this man coming; and the children have been sent to the door to call him. He sees them beckoning and is hurrying towards them.

He is carrying for sale small playthings for children and various small objects made of thin metal, such as little Buddhas, animal faces and lucky charms, which mothers stitched on to children's hats and slippers. He also has a plait of coloured tapes for sewing on aprons or similar purposes; and in his box he has many things more.

The Itinerant Salesman

EVERY ITINERANT SALESMAN has his special and familiar means of announcing his coming. This man carries a metal ring, which he twists to attract the attention of housewives who may be in need of the many household articles for sewing and mending clothes which he carries on his back. The character in the middle of the rattle is a simple way of writing *Xing* (Hsing), indicating popularity and prosperity; like so many Chinese words it has several meanings, but conveys a feeling of happy success.

The Cloth Vendor

THE VENDOR OF CLOTH is a popular street trader. Women bargain with him, and conveniently obtain the commonly used materials, mostly made of cotton, and black or undyed, either natural or bleached, or various shades of blue. Although he may unroll and spread out his wares for a customer to see, feel and depreciate as she haggles, before he leaves every bundle is neatly made up and stacked on his shoulder board, secured by the strap which he holds in his hand.

Although the street seller may carry some simple patterned material, for more expensive cloth and for silks it is necessary to visit a shop, where young attendants, watched by the proprietor, will open before you roll after roll from the store.

The Sharman

ONLY ONCE DID I SEE the sharman or *duan gong*. To me he was picturesque in his symbolic garments, with the circle containing the two intermingling elements, the yin and the yang, representing the vital essence of the universe itself, the absolute, the great ultimate; those female and male principles which, blending in limitless permutations, yielded the sun, moon and stars. To others he was a figure of dread or of hope; having power to give protection against evil, to cast out devils, and to give charms to bring good fortune, or ill.

The women and children standing around him, watched every movement, but gave no indication of their own feelings. He was standing before a row of lit candles: an odd number so as to make them effective. There were also a bowl of water and long sticks of incense. He was waving aloft a sheaf of burning paper held in one hand; in the other he rattled his circular wand as he shouted incantations.

Round the yin and the yang were the eight diagrams of broken and unbroken lines, associated with the Dao, and which through the law of changes gave rise to the ten thousand objects of which this world is made. On his head was the ten petal diadem with the symbols of divination.

When I asked the artist about him his eyes twinkled. He assured me that it cost only a copper to cast out a devil from an ordinary person; but the devils of the rich were much more reluctant to leave their comfortable homes, so the cost was much greater.

端公禳鬼圖
鄉僻之人多信此法以禳病

85

Pigs for Market

EVERY DAY IN THE EARLY MORNING, from the lane by the university, came a constant squeaking of wheelbarrow wheels, as pigs were taken to be slaughtered, so that the people of Chengdu could have their pork.

These black pigs came from a multitude of farms scattered over the plain, and set off in small droves, little boys walking with them, carrying buckets of water, which they used to sprinkle the pigs to keep them cool. I used to think it cruel the way the pigs' long ears were pierced and tied over their heads, until a drover explained that the ears were so long they hung over the eyes, so that the pigs could see nothing unless the ears were held back.

Eventually the pigs grew too weary to walk. It was the moment for which the following wheelbarrow men were waiting. The pigs were turned upside down, fastened to bamboo cradles lined with straw, and given a ride for the rest of their journey. Putting the pigs on the barrows caused the most piercing chorus of squeals; but these soon ceased, and there were only occasional grunts as they continued on their way.

Slaughtering

SLAUGHTERING IS NEVER PLEASANT. This black pig has had its throat cut, the blood being collected in the wooden bowl. Every bit of the pig is used; some of its bristles may have found their way to Europe, as they used to be exported from Chengdu for making tooth-brushes.

Seeing this picture reminds me of how, in April 1925, we were present at the spring sacrifice to Confucius. Around 4 a.m., for everything had to be completed before dawn, we gathered in the lovely temple, secluded behind its yellow walls. At the end of an inner courtyard, the trees mysterious in the light of red lanterns, on a raised terrace, was the shrine containing the tablet to Confucius. It was approached by a central dragon slope, flanked by steps on each side for human beings.

The sacrifice was made by the Governor of the Province. Resplendent in top hat and morning coat, he made the series of three bows, nine in all, at stated times before the tablet of the Sage, and offered prayer on behalf of the people. Students from the Confucian School played antiphonally, some on metal instruments, others on jade; two other groups postured in ancient dance.

Before the altar, in the centre, was the carcase of a young bull, as near a perfect one as could be found; to its left a goat, and to the right a pig, all on frames as in the picture, only higher. They had been ritually killed the previous day. Before each of two other altars, on which were tablets of Confucian scholars, a pig and a goat were stretched.

When the ceremony was over, the sacrificial beasts were to be divided and sent to government offices in the city.

The Meat Vendor

MEAT COULD BE BOUGHT FROM STREET SELLERS, who carried long pieces of pork dangling from the end of their poles. They stopped for customers as they went from street to street. When asked, the vendor would cut off a strip or a piece, and put through it one of the bamboo slivers hung from his pole, so that the purchaser could carry it home.

Meat was relatively expensive, and few people could eat it daily. For some it was a weekly event, but for the very poor meat could rarely be eaten, except on feast days.

Before it was cooked the meat was chopped up in the kitchen into pieces of convenient size for eating with chopsticks. Knives were not used at table and forks were unknown.

The Butcher's Shop

THE BEST SELECTION OF MEAT was to be found in the butchers' shops. It was invariably pork, except in the larger establishments, where goat and beef were for sale, especially if Moslem customers were expected. There were no joints as we know them, but pieces were selected and cut from bisected pig.

The price of the day was an important matter, discussed with neighbours and with those who had already been shopping before a purchase was made: to the housewife every *cash*★ was important. The shop in the picture is drawing attention by its bold notice to the offer of meat at 1,200 *cash* for a catty: an attractive bargain for any keen shopper. But she must be wary and look again; in lighter strokes the characters really announce the price as 1,599 – which is no better, and may indeed be dearer than anywhere else.

★ A lead and copper coin of low denomination usually with a square hole in the centre.

Transporting Rice

AN IMPORTANT EVENT FOR ALL HOUSEHOLDS who could afford it was the purchase of new rice when the harvest was over. Some arranged for regular deliveries throughout the year, or if they possessed a large bin, for sufficient to fill it. The rice was brought from the farm or the dealer in sacks which could be delivered in several ways; one at each end of his pole by carriers or on one or more wheelbarrows; or sometimes, as in the picture, on the back of an ox. While the animal bore its full load of rice, it was the man who carried food for the beast, in a long sack, twisted in the middle to allow a satisfactory weight on his head.

The arrival of rice was an important domestic event: it had to be measured, stored and paid for. It was poured into a wooden measure, holding exactly one bushel, any excess being levelled off with greatest care. Then bushel by bushel it was carried to the store, which had been carefully cleaned, hoping to keep the new rice free from the insects which often infested the old. The number of bushels was carefully checked, either by putting aside a stick for each one, or by adding a stroke to *zheng* (which means correct or exact), each completed character representing five bushels (一 丁 干 正 正).

Finally with the help of an abacus, the account was calculated. Then payment was made; in those days, in silver dollars, each one being carefully rung to see that it was true and not debased or forged. If the former, its true value had to be discussed and agreed; if the latter, the coin was discarded.

The Stone Mason

AROUND CHENGDU THE GRAVES WERE USUALLY SIMPLE. The mounds of earth over the massive wooden coffins were sometimes covered with mortar, and had a stone, such as the mason is shaping, in which was cut the name and dates of the deceased, the characters when new often coloured red. The family graves were often clustered together near the farms, so that there was a sense that the living and dead shared in the toil. For the rich there might be more elaborate graves, on plots that the family owned in the country; for all it was important to find and if necessary, to purchase, a propitious site for the grave likely to bring good fortune to the family.

Every year at the Spring Festival it was the custom to visit the graves, tidy them up, and tend to the welfare of the ancestor by sending to him, in the spirit world, cash, servants and probably a new house, the paper replicas being transferred by burning. It was then time for a family picnic, the dead having partaken of the spiritual essence of the food the living had brought.

Customs have greatly changed since the coming of the People's Republic. Land is needed if the people are to be fed; instead of clusters of graves round the farms, the dead are buried deeply so that the ground above them can be tilled; and cremation has been introduced for urban dwellers.

The Mandarin Express

THIS TYPE OF CHAIR WAS A MANDARIN EXPRESS, with elegant curved wooden poles, in which officials, their wives or concubines used to be carried importantly through the streets. This is a form used in summer; in winter the light chair is enclosed to keep the occupant warm. The carriers were dressed in uniform, a favourite colour being light blue, trimmed with white. Some business managers used red, with the name of the firm on the men's backs. On their feet they wear straw sandals to prevent them from slipping. Two men carry and proceed at a slow, steady run. In the picture a third man is lifting the chair from the front man's shoulders and will put it on his own, the pace hardly slackening. The free man will run alongside, until it is time to change with the carrier at the back, who will be free until he changes with the front man. In the case of very important officials, four or even more carriers were used, so that the changes were more frequent, the speed greater, and the prestige enhanced.

The lady is smoking her water pipe, but officials usually closed their eyes, as if asleep. This was to avoid meeting an acquaintance for then the chair would have had to stop and be put down, for unless he was someone of very low status it would have been the greatest discourtesy to speak from a height. Equals should stand on the same level of ground.

One of the pranks the artist played as a boy was to watch for some official approaching. Then, from a secure hiding place, to shout very loudly, awakening the official who, in fear, would think he was attacked by robbers. The small boy then escaped before he could be caught.

An Everyday Chair

FOR VISITS TO SHOPS, or friends and relations in the city, you called two men with an everyday chair. They would carry you at a quick walk, wherever you wanted to go. They waited for hire by the side of the streets or ambling along in the crowds. The front man would lower his end of the poles to the ground and in you would step. Then with a bit of a struggle, he lifts it up again, puts the poles on his shoulders and away you go; but there was no relief for the carriers until the end of the journey.

The chair was light in weight, the frame of bamboo, often covered with oil-cloth. There was a curtain in front, in case it was raining. In a very old chair, the bottom occasionally gave way, to the great embarrassment of the occupant and the joy of observers.

Long Distance Travel

FOR JOURNEYS OUTSIDE THE CITY, a three man chair was often used. The poles were adjusted so that the back carrier was considered to have a fair share of the weight. After about two hundred or so steps, the front carrier would call and the chair stop; then the second man rested it on the upright pole he is carrying. The shoulder pole is changed over from one shoulder to the other and the chair proceeds. Eventually the chair is put down while the three men rest.

For a journey of several days, or if the passenger was heavy, a four man chair was required, the two men at the back being linked in the same manner as the two front men in the picture. This means that the third man has no view of the road ahead. One of the few pleasures of a mode of travel which involved hard labour for one's fellow men, and often shoulders with festering sores, was to listen to the rhymed couplets, usually humorous, by means of which the first man warned of dangers ahead and the third man acknowledged that he understood.

For puddles in the road: 'Here a river, a river doth flow,' and the third man responded: 'Each for himself must over it go.' Children were often in the way: 'Little plaything, cries at night,' with the reply: 'Tell his ma to hold him tight.' Or, more conventionally: 'Cloud in the sky': then, 'Below a person close by.' When the path was dangerous: 'Steep slope, slippery dip' with the encouraging reply: 'He who has legs will not slip.' At the end of the day, when the men were tired, humour vanished and clever extemporising ended.

The New Rickshaw

WHEN FIRST WE WENT TO CHENGDU there were no rickshaws. The only wheeled vehicles were wheelbarrows. Then, quite suddenly, rickshaws began to appear. Wheels were imported; and the chairs and shafts were made locally by the clever craftsmen who were ready to try their skill at anything. They were still a novelty when the artist drew this: he numbered it 14!

Private rickshaws also arrived for officials and important people. They were more elaborate, with pneumatic tyres, shining black mudguards, comfortable seats and efficient hoods. They had lamps, carefully polished, and above all a bell, worked by pressing with a foot. Impatiently and ceaselessly it would ring, as these influential men or their ladies were drawn by smart pullers, threading their way through the crowded streets. They introduced a new element into the medley of Chengdu street noises.

To accommodate the rickshaws a programme of street widening was commenced and wheelbarrows whose narrow wheels were damaging the new streets were barred from the city. Before long still wider streets had to be made, to make way for the motor vehicles which came from the coast.

One of the oddest sights I saw in China was in a village not far from Chengdu: in a rickshaw made entirely of wood, including the wheels which were solid and of the usual size, was sitting an old Daoist priest, in full regalia, his face quite impassive. The puller could hardly make the thing move, despite the fact that a small boy was pushing.

Child Transport

THERE WAS ANOTHER WAY OF TRAVELLING – if you were small enough. Moving house, and the grandson, too young to walk, is carried in a basket. He is waving a rattle, and his hair is done in a popular style for baby boys: a little patch left in the middle, the rest being shaved; the hair, bound tightly with thread, standing up straight.

In the other basket are some of the family possessions: a pig-skin box, containing neatly folded best clothes and any valuables because it has a lock. On the box a bamboo mat on which to sleep, and above that a padded quilt.

When the carrier needs to rest he balances the carrying pole on the stick he is holding, one of the baskets resting on the ground. The stick is also useful to help with the balance: he gives it a swing and a flourish as he jogs along.

鄉老搬家圖
省事鋪陳
幼子一肩挑
一九三〇 子丹作於成都東郊之外

107

The Sugar-cane Seller

An example of the artist's difficulty with perspective – and yet the picture is rich in detail: the sticks of purple sugar-cane below the stall; the pieces cut ready for sale, ringed in the conventional manner, but kept fresh by using the brush to sprinkle water from the small bucket. When customers are few and the seller has time, he cuts out a highly simplified form of the character *shou*, meaning long life, in the middle purple ring of each piece. Perhaps it counteracts the effect of the rather doubtful water he uses!

On most days the road near the stall is littered with fibre, spat out after chewing the chunks which strong teeth tear from the cane. During the days of Chiang Kai Shek's New Life Movement a futile attempt was made to prevent this. 'But what can we do?' a chewer expostulated. 'It is impossible to swallow the stuff!'

Milking

CHENGDU COWS, BROWN IN COLOUR, were not bred for their milk, but as farm animals and, as there was a considerable Moslem community, for meat. This meant that we were not condemned solely to pork and occasional goat, but could buy beef if we wished. We also needed milk, especially for our children; but as the Chinese disliked cow's milk, declaring it 'heating' with bad effects on their health, it was often difficult to obtain.

Some westerners financed Chinese willing to keep cows for their milk. At one time the milk with which we were supplied got thinner and thinner, and I believed that water was added. A complaint produced an invitation to watch the milking. The two cows were kept in a small straw shed on waste ground; they rarely went out, but were fed on grass cut by small children, baskets on backs, armed with sharp 'grass-knives'. 'Looking after cows dirties one so,' the milkman explained: the filthy surroundings at least confirmed how right we were to strain away the grime, and boil every drop of milk that came into the house.

I found no fault with the milking; but a Chinese colleague nudged me and said: 'Look again!' Up the milkman's sleeve was a bottle of water, its cork with a carefully made groove. But how could a relatively wealthy foreigner get angry at the ingenuity of someone living below the poverty line, striving to make a living for himself and his family?

In time all this was changed. A good foreign bull was imported, and now any Chinese children who wish may drink high standard cow's milk.

Grinding Soya Beans – 1

THESE THREE MEN ARE TURNING the millstone to crush soya beans. At the back of the shop sacks of beans were piled high. There was always a half-circle of children gazing in through the open shutters. There was something fascinating about the way the yellow beans, which had first been soaked, were fed in through a hole in the top stone and then yielded the white milk which flowed out to be collected in a large pan. The men turned the heavy upper stone slowly, with great deliberation – anti-clockwise, of course, in the Chinese way.

Some of the milk was collected, chiefly to be sent to the hospital, for an attempt was being made at that time to use it for small babies and children, as cow's milk was not available. However, most of the milk, by the addition of alum, was turned into bean curd. This was strained through muslin lined wooden boxes, with holes in the bottom, the curd being left and cut into the familiar white squares. It was this vegetable protein that enabled the labouring Chinese to accomplish their amazing hard work.

Grinding Soya Beans – 2

As OFTEN HAPPENED, there were several shops close together engaged in the same occupation. This is a simpler mill for grinding beans, worked by one man while his wife adds the soya beans which have been soaked in the earthenware basin. She also helps to see that the stone turns easily. The milk is collected in a wooden bucket.

The bean curd, made by the addition of alum, may be eaten in various ways, either alone or as part of other dishes, fried or boiled. Condiments are added to give it flavour, especially red pepper. The capsicum is ground with oil, which makes it more effective, and to me was frighteningly hot.

There is also a variety of bean curd which has been allowed to ferment, growing long hairs of mould. Chinese who have been abroad liked to compare it with the riper cheeses of the West, about which some strange tales were told.

Powdering Rice

THE FIRST MONTH OF THE LUNAR CALENDAR was always an exciting time. At the beginning was New Year itself; then on the 15th day there was a special festival when people visited their friends and enjoyed eating *tang yuan*, a kind of dumpling: the *tang* meaning hot, and *yuan* the season of the year. These white balls, the size of a small plum, were quite plain, but served surrounded by sweetened water from a bowl and eaten with chopsticks. There was some boasting, and competition, among the young about how many they had managed to eat.

The man in the picture is powdering rice for making the balls. The glutinous variety is used as it enables the *tang yuan* to keep their round shape.

椿湯元粉岩

一九三〇年　俞平丹作

The Street Kitchen

MANY CHINESE FIND SNACKS IRRESISTIBLE. These street sellers attracted many customers: the food looked good, the taste was satisfying, the smell was good too – especially from the boiling soup in which the noodles have been cooked. The bucket hanging from the carrying pole is the washing-up bowl: there is a well-used rag somewhere to give the bowls and chopsticks an extra wipe between customers. In the open drawer there is a supply of bean curd; and to season it, soy sauce, red peppers, ginger, spices and tasty pickles.

The Evening Restaurant

IN THE EVENING, on the university campus, a number of itinerant restaurants used to gather around the entrances to the various hostels where the students lived. After an evening of study, before going to bed, it was pleasant to buy a bowl of noodles, piping hot, with good tasty soup, well flavoured with the condiments of your choice. It was said that the only place where the menu never varied was at the women's hostel. The request was always for noodles, red with the hottest peppers. It might be warming on cold winter nights, but hardly my own idea of the best way to induce untroubled sleep.

Seller of Fried Snacks

TO COME ACROSS A SNACK BAR, dangling from the ends of a carrier's shoulder pole, is to feel immediate hunger. Partly it is the smell, also the sight and the memory of past indulgence: for some it is almost compulsory to stop him and taste his wares. Children, if they themselves have insufficient coppers, will plead with their parents to buy a bowl of 'carrier's noodles.'

The man in the drawing specialises in fried snacks, such as small fried flat cakes and twists of dough. They had little flavour and often were tough; but my Chinese friends liked them. Also they enjoyed chewing them at breakfast with their rice gruel, especially when soya bean milk was added.

Another popular itinerant sold dumplings, kept hot in round steamers made of thin wood or shiny tin. These *baozi* were of two kinds, both made from wheat flour, and steamed. One sort was filled with various kinds of meat; and the other, marked with a red spot, had a sweet filling. *Baozi* may be enjoyed at any time and are often given to guests while preparations for a meal are being completed.

Fried Biscuits

THESE ROUND FRIED BISCUITS or cakes were popular. You could buy them from street stalls or from the baker in his shop. They were welcome, if one was a farmer, to chew on the way home after market, or if one needed a snack when the loads were heavy to carry: they were frequently eaten for breakfast. They were made from wheat flour, quite plain, lightly fried, crisp but without much taste, rather like a water-biscuit. They reminded me slightly of girdle cakes, but the pan is larger than the round plate used in the north of England for making a single cake over the kitchen fire; also the Chinese cakes are made tasty, and also nutritious, by being sprinkled before cooking with sesame or other seeds.

Filial Instruction

THIS ROUGH SKETCH was to drive home some points made by Yu Zidan as teacher, who had been discussing the place of the individual in the family. The father is instructing the son, but pointing to the old grandfather, now deceased. The individual could find significance only within the family setting. He was a link in a chain, which stretched back into the past and, hopefully, would extend far into the future. His motive in life should be to bring no disgrace to those who have gone; and himself to do nothing of which his descendants might be ashamed.

Characteristic of that period, when old traditions still lingered, no mention was made of women. Girls hardly counted, for after marriage they belonged to another family. They were the vessels through whom the male line of the family continued. It is remarkable how quickly these attitudes have changed. As Mao Zedong pointed out, women hold up half the sky: the equality of their benefits and rights with men is recognised throughout the People's Republic.

The Teller of Fortunes

THERE USED TO BE VARIOUS GENTLEMEN, who sat at little tables in strategic places. They were writers and readers of letters for the illiterate, and tellers of fortunes, determining lucky days for weddings, funerals, and business or family ventures. The space between the inner and outer city gates was a popular place, along with the changers of silver dollars into 100 and 200 *cash*★ pieces. Some were in their unshuttered homes, depending on the weather and on their status.

This man, who looks like a survivor of the scholar-gentry, has a book, and is doubtless knowledgeable about the influence of wind and water, and the yin and the yang. He is wearing old Chinese spectacles, the case hanging from his clothing. If he met you on the street, he would raise his glasses as a sign of respect. By his side there is a small altar. The central bowl contains sand, in which to put sticks of incense, and two brass or pewter candlesticks, each shaped as a conventionalised character for *shou*, meaning longevity. Behind these is the central tablet, *Sheng Yu*, Imperial Edict. On its right are listed four of the five human relationships: ruler and minister; father and son; older and younger brother; and friend and friend – but that of husband and wife is left out. On the other side are the names of the moral principles on which good relationships are based: propriety or ceremony; righteousness; honesty; and a sense of shame.

★ See page 92

The Student Actor

STUDENTS IN CHINA WERE, in certain ways, different from those I had taught in England. In general terms the Chinese worked harder, but one had to remember that they were selected from a very much larger number of applicants; they could remember almost every word I ever said: the consequence of memory training through learning to read and write their own language; and all were sensitive to ridicule, so that the wise teacher in China was never sarcastic, and did his best to preserve the self-respect of his students.

In the West, children are frequently threatened with smacks or a thrashing; in China the sanction imposed from the earliest age was: 'People will laugh at you!' Its effect was apparent in many situations. 'Don't laugh at me' pleads the student attempting a chemical experiment for the first time. 'It is laughable' was the immediate defence, forestalling ridicule which might have come from some thoughtless word or action. 'I must play behind a curtain,' says the violin player. 'The audience might laugh and then I could not continue.'

This explains, I believe, why everyone enjoys so much the performance shown in the picture. The young man at the table, wearing a mask to show he is acting and not a genuine fool may not speak a word, but accepts and acts out the situation which, with great skill, his hidden accomplice describes. His folly, the dilemmas he brings on himself, his stupidity as he faces humorous situations, bring delight to all who are watching.

The Professional Actor

WHILE THE PREVIOUS PICTURE on p. 131 shows a student performance, this entertainer is much more professional; you know he is playing the part of a fool, by the white mask he wears on his face. In the illustration of the two students, the accomplice, who does all the talking, is crouching beside the performer, to whom the words are supposed to apply. He is not supposed to be seen by the audience. In this picture the witty talker is hidden behind the table.

Although I could enjoy a good deal of the fun, much of it was far beyond me. The Chinese language is full of ambiguities: each word may have various meanings which depend on the context. There are many allusions, impossible to appreciate without a knowledge of classical Chinese. This is one reason why translations from the Chinese often vary so greatly, particularly of poems.

The Diabolo Seller

THE DIABOLO SELLER WAS ALWAYS ENJOYABLE, for he himself was so skilful as he demonstrated his wares, spinning his double top and throwing it into the air. As children stood watching, they wondered if they could spin a diabolo as well as he was doing – or perhaps even better. Every year, for a season, it was their popular game.

Although the skill is beyond him until he is older, the little boy is delighted to see the top spinning. Note the hair standing straight up through the gap in his animal hat, and the cut-away pants – ever-readies, as western mothers called them.

Dough Models

THIS MAN, AMBLING ALONG in search of a place to set up his stand, makes little things out of dough. He carries his materials in the box on his back. He will take a lump of coloured dough in his fingers, press it and twist, sometimes using a bamboo splinter or a wire around which to build. He cuts and he scrapes and adds small pieces of coloured dough or paste until little figures appear as you watch: animals, dragons, men and women well known in story. Children and grown-ups gather to watch him at work, for pressure never seems too great to prevent people having some time to spare.

捏五彩麪人賣
以謀生活之小藝家

The Toymaker

STREET SELLERS WERE VERY OFTEN most skilful and fascinating to watch. This man was a toy maker, but his products were simpler and not so artistic as those made from dough (see page 137). He took his material in a lump from a pan, kept warm by charcoal, and inserting a reed began to blow. As the mass enlarged he shaped it with hands and fingers until an animal or other toy seemed by magic to form, to the delight of those who were watching who would speculate in excited voices about what he was making. He added colour, and the reed remained a useful handle to stick on his frame of goods for sale, or for a child to hold if he had bought one.

When I asked him what they were made from, he would not tell me, but politely resorted to the acceptable excuse when asked awkward questions by a foreigner. 'I am sorry, but I cannot understand what you are saying.' I think they were mainly made of sugar, boiled to the right consistency, perhaps with the addition of cereal.

Musicians

THE ARTIST MUST HAVE COME ACROSS this pair of entertainers at a concert. They are both dressed up for the occasion. He has the character for *shou*, longevity, on his clothing. This is a very popular motif and is commonly woven into black silk damask, which shows by the reflection of light. It is used for the more expensive jackets and gowns of better-off women and men.

He is playing the fiddle, *hu qin* (胡琴) which is very much liked throughout China. It is so called because it originally came from the northern tribes, the Tartars and Mongols. This is the two-string instrument, the *er hu* (二胡). She plays the castanets and the flat-drum or *gu*. Both are singing, possibly songs from Sichuan opera.

The woman's hair is dressed in the usual manner for an older person. She is sitting on a chair which is not very comfortable but of traditional design. In the back is set a piece of polished marble, chosen for its pleasing natural pattern of varied colours.

The Four-stringed Fiddle

ANOTHER PAIR OF ENTERTAINERS with a younger woman judging from her hair style. This gives a clearer picture of the 'fiddle from the northern tribes', but in this case it is one with four strings. There are fiddles of various kinds and sizes, the drums, or sound boxes, varying in diameter up to a foot or so, corresponding to a bass or double-bass. Sometimes a number of players will perform together; and an orchestra may include other instruments such as the *di*, or short flute, made of bamboo, or the *xiao*, a longer bamboo flute. At the time of the Tang Dynasty, it was declared that stringed instruments were not equal to the bamboo or reed and the latter were surpassed by the human voice.

The early story of Chinese music is shrouded in delightful mystery, after the time when the legendary Yellow Emperor, Huang-di, commanded his minister to cut bamboo tubes with which to imitate the notes of the phoenix; the male and the female birds sang alternately, the female replying to the notes of the male. The pentatonic scale was recognised by 400 B.C., modern music being established by the time of the Tang Dynasty, 618 A.D. Ancient books describe the five notes as being the essence of the five planets, expressed on earth as the soul of the five elements, and in man linked with his five organs.

The Mud and Water Worker

THE MUD AND WATER WORKER, as the plumber-cum-building repairer is realistically called, is on the way home from a job. He carries his ladder, his bucket of lime and the sieve for sifting the earth he uses. With his mattock he mixes the lime, earth and water until the consistency is right.

At first sight, some of the Chengdu dwellings remind the newcomer of the lath and plaster houses of England. He will discover that the laths are strips of stout bamboo, sharpened at each end, to fix into the beams which form the frames of the squares; the laths are then covered, both sides, with mortar and whitewashed.

To cut out a square, especially if weakened by age, is a favourite trick of thieves: a much easier way of gaining entry than through the carefully locked wooden doors.

As the beams from which the house is built are often the shape of the · trees from which they are cut, and vary considerably, it is said that it is impossible to make an accurate plan of a house until the building is finished.

Whitewashing

THIS MUD AND WATER WORKER has mounted his precarious ladder so that he can whitewash the walls. Later he may go on to the roof, as heavy rains cause leaks, and the grey tiles will need re-setting. The curves at the corners of the roof add a touch of delight to many dwellings: as is well known they are designed so that evil spirits may slide off into space, should they land on the top of the house with intent to do mischief.

Like most walls around homes in the city, this one is topped with a design of intertwined flowers, made from roof tiles, in pairs, concave sides inwards and held in position by dabs of mortar. It is not only attractive to look at, but like most things in China has also a practical use: it is a most effective burglar alarm. The structure is so flimsy that anyone trying to climb over the wall will bring the tiles tumbling down with a crash, rousing the dogs, whose barking will spread from house to house, until the neighbourhood is wide awake and on the alert.

Sawing Planks

MANPOWER HAS ALWAYS BEEN CHINA'S greatest capital asset. A wood-yard, with a dozen or so pairs of men at work, slowly but surely sawing planks from great tree trunks drives this fact home: it is so different from the noisy mechanical sawmill where planks roll off seemingly in no time. Patiently, rhythmically, pulling and pushing, the Chengdu men talked as they worked, pausing to wedge up the sawn portion of a board to prevent the saw jamming.

I used to visit a wood-yard in search of sawdust for students to distil, but also to mix with coal-dust; moistened with the water in which rice has been boiled it makes excellent coal-balls, ensuring a glowing fire for cold winter evenings. Seeing my interest in the sawdust, a sawyer dug down into one of the piles, revealing the largest maggots I have ever seen. Pointing to his mouth, he repeated *hao chi, hao chi* – they are good to eat. My response, I am afraid, was to shiver.

Floating Timber

THERE WERE NO TREES IN CHENGDU except around the lovely temples, or in the more spacious courtyards, together with a few in private gardens. Also, there were very few in the country round about, apart from a few solitary giants on the tops of hills. These survived, partly because of magical powers they were supposed to possess, but chiefly because the old narrow paths led to them, and weary carriers could put down their loads and rest awhile in the shade. Through the generations, the people had denuded the land, partly for timber, but chiefly for firewood.

Trees and great beams were brought from the still forested mountains to the west, beyond the Chengdu plain. They came by raft in summer when the rivers were swollen. If they were needed in winter when the rivers were shallow, they were carried by men yoked together. Frequently there were eight carriers, a pair at each side at the front, with ropes passing under the wood, and a similar arrangement at the back. It was difficult for them along the old roads, but other traffic stood aside to let them pass, for it was a rule that simple loads always gave way to those that were more cumbersome.

The Cooper

A NUMBER OF THINGS HAD TO BE MADE FROM WOOD, such as this tub on which the cooper is at work. There are few articles, however, in the making of which bamboo does not play some part. Here the ropes are made of plaited bamboo; for smaller tubs strips of bamboo are sometimes wound round instead.

'Wash-foot-tub' was the name commonly used in Chengdu; this was an important use, but also clothes were washed in it, or small children given baths – and grown-ups may have used it too. The care of the feet was of prime importance for the toilers who walked many miles in a day. Neglect could encourage sores and incapacity. To wash feet, and enjoy the relief that it brought, was almost the first necessity when the day's work was over. After the last meal was prepared, and the weather allowed, our cook would relax in a bamboo chair in the garden, while his wife brought a bowl of hot water, and kneeling before him, rolled up the legs of his trousers, so that he could recover from the labour of buying and cooking food for a family from 'over the ocean'.

Plaiting Mats

THERE CANNOT HAVE BEEN A HOME IN CHENGDU without mats made from plaited bamboo. The largest were used for sunning rice to keep it free from moulds and insects. Small ones were used to sleep on: most cool and comfortable on the hot humid nights of summer. The humblest people, in their cramped homes, would spread mats on the bare earth floor, in an attempt to find a cool place; or on the hottest nights might take them outside to the courtyard, or unroll them by the side of the road.

One special use was as ceilings; below the bare tiles they gave a room a tidy appearance, cool from the sun-heated roof, and warmer in winter. In time, 'guests-who-live-up-above' would make their home on the matting, and when all was quiet one would hear the rats and their families scurrying about their business. When the matting gets old, fighting rodents have been known to fall through onto floors or perhaps onto beds. It was then time to pull down the old dusty matting, and call in a weaver to make and fit a new ceiling.

The Blacksmith

A BLACKSMITH AT WORK, some of the things he makes hung up behind him: choppers for meat and vegetables, knives, and tongs for arranging the charcoal as it glows in the open braziers with which rooms are heated. Beside him, at the right of the furnace, is the handle of the bellows which he works out and in until he obtains the heat he requires.

Sharpening Knives

A VEGETABLE CHOPPER being sharpened ready for sale. Bamboo sections make most useful containers: in this one is the oil for the stone. There is a weight at the end of the trestle-seat, helping to keep it balanced and steady.

The Tinsmith

PEWTER GOODS WERE IN COMMON USE – as vases, ornaments, but especially as vessels on family altars: bowls in which to stand sticks of incense, and holders for candles. The tinsmith here has all his simple equipment: the earthenware stove, using charcoal as fuel, for heating the tin and lead; the mould into which the molten metal is poured; the lathe, turned by the foot treadles, on which the smith removes any irregularities and smoothes his products.

錫匠作
一九三〇年，戚艶俞樣山
戴筆

Polishing Pewter

PEWTER ORNAMENTS HAVE A VERY HIGH POLISH WHEN NEW, but quickly tarnish in most households. When dull they remain somewhat attractive, like the ancient bronzes; for me it was the shape that specially pleased the eye. I was told that this man uses a little water on his wooden wheel to polish recently made pewter articles, but also rubs them with the leaves of a special tree; but Chinese housewives used very fine sand, made into a paste with a little soda.

A Craftsman

RAT TRAPS, BIRD CAGES, toys for the children, scoops for the kitchen, supports for flowers, and the skeletons of fans, which still needed to be papered over: what a joy it was to see and to use these handmade goods. If there were slight imperfections here and there, they served as a reminder that they were made by a craftsman, with none of the soulless perfection of machine-made goods.

The Chinese were skilled craftsmen, willing to attempt making the most intricate things with their fingers and simple tools. During the war with Japan, when we were in urgent need of precision balances for use in the Department of Chemistry, an amateur craftsman made several for us, using brass for the beams, and local agate for the knife edges. They proved to be the equal of some we had previously imported. From this small beginning a new industry was started, and 40 years later, is making balances and other scientific instruments as well.

Making Spirit Money

A mint, where currency is manufactured for dispatch to the spirit world. The money is made by stamping a piece of paper, on which nothing is printed, with a die which has a cutting edge, shaped as an incomplete circle, so that the disc, which represents a coin, remains attached. There are eight of these 'coins' on a piece of the locally made unbleached, unsized, grass-paper – like those in the picture. By burning, this imaginary money is transferred to the departed, either at funerals, or during visits to the graves, so that those who have gone may be kept in funds and will be able to purchase the things they need. Chengdu people were satisfied by this symbolic wealth; only the rich could afford the ostentatious printed paper money on some bank of the underworld, and the shiny model gold bars and silver sycee.

This money-maker lived in the lane near the university. He was following his father in the profession, and perhaps his grandfather too. So diligent had they been, so successful in business, that they had worn away the tree trunk they used as a block. A new one had just been purchased, but it was too tall, so that the operator had to stand on the counter to hammer out the money. The man told the artist: 'I hope that most of the tree will remain for my son to earn his livelihood on it.' No-one then realised the changes that soon were to come; the son was likely to find that the demand for his paper money had gone.

Bamboo Articles

THIS MAKER OF BAMBOO ARTICLES has all sorts of things for sale. As well as the baskets of various kinds, he carries a circular frame to put into a rice-steamer on which to cook *baozi*, the good-to-eat dumplings. He also has bamboo scrubbers to scrape out the iron cauldrons, or *guo* used in every home to fry or boil food. It was said at the time that almost every item of domestic need could be made from bamboo and the empty oil tins in which paraffin had been imported into Sichuan from the coast, so that people were able to have brighter lights, instead of relying on the small smoky flames from wicks dipped in rape-seed oil.

Iron Cooking Pans

THIS IS A LOAD OF IRON COOKING PANS. They are so typically Chinese that everyone calls them *guo* (锅), especially as there is no concise English name. No household is without one or more. They are made in various sizes and may be supported on a cooking range of bricks and mortar or cement over an elaborate grate; or the grate may be quite simple, set in mud and mortar, sometimes in an old kerosene tin. Small stoves are often surrounded by a woven bamboo frame. On pages 73 and 75 a *guo* is being used to boil water for reeling silk.

The *guo* is used for preparing all manner of food by boiling or frying; and is covered by a wooden lid to keep in the heat. When rice is boiled a hard crust may stick to the hot bottom and is a special favourite. A steamer, usually of bamboo, may be placed over the boiling water to make steamed bread, dumplings and other special dishes. Around meal times, from the open homes, comes the sound of scraping and sizzling as the vegetables are stirred in the hot *guo* in a little rape or other oil, and the air becomes heavy with spiced and acrid fumes. In Chengdu the usual fuel was wood, leaves, grass or anything burnable that the women and girls could gather with their bamboo rakes.

There is no doubt that the carrier needed a rest, for the iron goods are heavy. He has made his own cheroot from a tobacco leaf, and his bamboo pipe is of the right size to slip under his belt when he is ready to proceed on his journey..

The Fruit Seller

SICHUAN IS RICH IN FRUITS, and this man, dressed in his winter clothing, is tempting customers with his sweet and juicy mandarin oranges. In his beautifully made baskets he carries a further supply. On one of the trays are halves and quarters, ready for those who cannot afford an entire fruit. When he has time he peels some oranges, ready for instant eating. The skin when dry, is good for burning with the grass and leaves when cooking food.

Fruit, whether sold like this, or from shops or stalls, is always clean and attractively arranged. As there was no refrigeration, and methods of preservation were unreliable, the varieties of fruit on the market varied with the seasons. Oranges, both mandarin and tight skin, were particularly sweet and refreshing – more seeds but more tasty than many highly cultivated western varieties. Persimmons, rich in vitamin C, were always attractive, although the unripe fruit was too astringent with tannin except for medicinal use. It was customary to ripen the fruit by inserting small twigs, which were often far from clean. Pears were magnificent to look at, but, surprisingly for the westerner, were crisp and watery: when peeled and coated with honey they changed almost entirely into ambrosial syrup. Local apples were as tasteless as cotton wool, but were rapidly being replaced by western varieties. The peach, symbol of long life, was always popular, as were apricots and the pumeloes with their giant segments.

In summer, the seller, dressed only in vest and trousers, offered slices of various kinds of melon – sought after by the thirsty and, in those days, by a multitude of flies.

The Postman

THE POSTMAN OF THOSE TIMES wore a uniform of green, his legs bound in puttees. The envelope he brandishes was the only kind then in general use; it needed paste to stick down the small flap, unless it was sealed with the postage stamps (which also needed paste). The address is written on the right by the sender; the name of the person to whom it is going is, politely, in large characters on the middle strip of red; on the left the sender's name and address, written small.

The postal service was a most successful organisation. At the beginning of the period, when these pictures were drawn, it took about three weeks for a letter from Chengdu to reach England, going speedily (we then thought) by train across Siberia. We considered we were lucky if we received a reply to a letter within two months.

The Medicine Seller

THE CHINESE ARE GREAT MEDICINE EATERS, and Chengdu was a place through which many of the old traditional herbs passed on their way to all parts of China, and abroad to wherever Chinese live. Many medicinal plants grow on the mountain sides and in the valleys to the west of the Chengdu plain, and in the regions that stretch between Sichuan and Tibet. The plants, their leaves or roots, are collected chiefly in spring and then carried across the plain by lines of carriers jogging along together.

Born of the experience of many centuries, there was great faith in Chinese medicine. A woman graduate of our medical school told me: 'For myself I always take Chinese medicine and feel that western treatment is superior only in surgery'; but she had been conditioned by her training, for she admitted: 'when my children are ill I always use western medicines.'

This old man is specialising in dog-skin plasters. The little black patches, with the dab of ointment on them, are freed from the paper backing and then put on sores or boils. The old gentleman keeps warm in his winter clothes and, instead of using a carrying pole, shoves his little cart which is distinctive and easier for him to manage. He trundles it through the streets, pausing here and there to sell his wares, and give advice on common ailments.

The Dragons Backbone

THESE TWO MEN WORKING ON THE DRAGONS BACKBONE, chatting together as they raise water to irrigate their fields, are symbolic of the period to which these pictures belong. There was a certain satisfaction to be found in work, whether in the small home industries or in making and then selling wares on the streets. There was little sense of oppression, of being bound by a rigid discipline. The tailor's small boys could stop their stitching to watch a dog fight; the weaver, hearing the sound of voices, could put down his shuttle and go to see what the talk was about; even the fishmonger, a rather pugnacious man, could leave his fish for a few moments to join in a wordy battle.

This period was in many ways the last of the 'old days', although they could hardly be called 'good', for there was too much misery, chiefly caused by poverty, malnutrition and ill-health; yet they were relatively good compared with the days that were to follow, after Japan invaded China, and run-away inflation brought fear throughout the land, with a government demoralised and incapable of ruling. It was Mao Zedong, his colleagues and those who rallied round them, who brought new hope, but also the realisation that if the many millions were to be adequately fed, and China enabled to take her rightful place in the world, production must be increased, and larger, more efficient, industries be established to replace such as the artist has painted for us.

So the days of these two men, gossiping as they work the treadmill, are numbered. Now it is electricity that pumps the water to irrigate the fields.